Praise for Evan Dekens

"In this gorgeous, gripping collection, Evan Dekens lovingly guts nostalgia, refusing truck with its belief in a superior—or at least simpler—past to which we might return and, so, regain our innocence. Or hurt less. Or find hope. Instead, Dekens returns us to sites of loss, to emptied places, in order to recount precisely what can no longer be found there—and what never could. Perhaps we haunt memory, this work suggests, as a means of avoiding the unbearable (because unrevivable, unrevisable) past and the devastating (because already evaporating) present. Here is a speaker who doesn't engage in such fantasies. Instead, in lyric both dreamy and sharp, he returns, clear eyed, to historic and personal sites of violence and erasure and inhabits now after aching now, elegizing precisely all that is about to disappear, which is, of course, everything. If there is recompense, it is language itself and the tenderness, the attention, the wish for connection that it evokes. These are wise and tender and unflinching poems. This is a stunning debut."
-Melissa Crowe, winner of the Iowa Poetry Prize for *Lo*

"*Anatomies of Disappearance* by Evan Dekens is a collection of clouds and stars. Milky and see-through. Heavy from what can feel like the unanswerable everything-the stinging noticings about class, race, family, place, history, and love-yet, light, too, from gentle word weaving that offers breath and translucency. And then there is blue. Dekens braids into these poems, the color of the sky, both night and day. As I read this work, I think of Maggie Nelson's *Bluets* and Imani Perry's *Back in Blue: How a Color Tells the Story of My People*. Like these writers, Dekens reminds us: literature can tell the story of a color and can embody it, too. There

are borders and blue. Rivers and blue. Bleeding and blue. *Anatomies of Disappearance* is a rich, sensual exploration of what may matter to bodies and souls as they move through time. As they take up space in homes and lands both understood and misunderstood. As they yield to the power of trees and rivers and sun. Angels, too."
-Kathy Curto, NYT author and professor of creative writing at Montclair State University

Anatomies of Disappearance

Evan Dekens

APRIL GLOAMING

Winner of the
Apogee Poetry Chapbook Award

Publisher's Cataloguing-in-Publication Data

Dekens, Evan
  Anatomies of disappearance / written by Evan Dekens
  ISBN: 978-1-953932-35-8

1. Poetry: General 2. Poetry: American - General I. Title II. Author

Library of Congress Control Number: 2025931878

Contents

For C—, the south, and all the rivers that run between.

Segregated

with dioxin

Something happened beside the once blue river
that curves like a long vein along this state.

The snare rises, then slips, to a deadbolt click
of cries closed by miles and miles
of ocean and bone and nowhere.

I drive each day between cities
over a border we can't utter.
A sealed, blue curve running through
white skin.

If this state were a body,
it would be tattooed with names

so small and crowded, they'd flow like a black
river, leading into the sea
of what and whose histories
have been kept from me.

The History Lesson

My first real winter was a blade.
I smoked frost against the bark of backwoods.
The men I knew wore their bodies
like lead x-ray vests. Their eyes did not grow.

In school, they told us history is all we have.
The record of existence.
We took pictures of our bodies,
afraid they might disappear.

Your mouth is a blade, I wrote.
How can you kiss anyone with a blade for a mouth?

I loved a quiet girl with large eyes,
skin white as a pill.
She dreamt only of the miracles
knives cannot perform
and wore a metal heart
on a chain necklace.

For years afterward, I kept my body concealed
in a small wooden box on the sill.

I prayed that it might be polished with moonlight
until it became a life.

Love Poem with Entropy

Say all things, atom by atom,
disappear without exception.

My father's little white car parked out back
chipping from rust and wind.

This arm I'm holding like a seatbelt
drawn over my chest, keeping me rooted to the sheets.

I remember bells & blue poured from my lips
when low Carolina light fell on us from between the shades.

Covered in sex and blue sheets and the blue sound
of starlings I would never hear again. Blue is what bleeds

from threadbare shirts once new like fresh skin.
From the end of dreams as they dim into morning,

where I am in a river of blue among long-gone uncles
and cousins, crawling like a city toward the bluffs

where my mother's face and my father's, and all the faces
that have ever flashed across my life, end.

As We Begin Our Descent

After Carlos Drummond DeAndrade

The silver-haired woman next to me
takes my hand and whispers: *Simon,
we've made it, we're finally here.*

To the other passengers of the plane
we must look like relatives,
one generation clutching another
on our way back home.

And two hours behind the holiday,
with the runway speckled by cones
of lavender light,
I wish it were true.

That it were somehow you next to me,
floral silk shirt clinging in the half-dark
to your kindly halted frame,
I could ask you how I came to be.

How you escaped the soap factories
and bricked suburbs, their slanted roads,
the honey crisp fog spilling from
red pitchers of wine-soaked peaches.

I feel the woman's wrinkled
palm on mine, her pale raisin skin
like a hand from the past,
a dream erased when I say:
Simon, no, I'm not Simon,
but you can still hold my hand.

A film falls from her eyes as she says
sorry, she's come to New York to see
her granddaughter for the first time.
She asks if I have a grandmother.

I say no before I correct myself.
Yes, her name was Gloria,
I think, Gloria, Gloriana
Gloria, Gloria, Gloria.

Below, Manhattan looks like a spent log
lit with windy embers, and I wonder
if, like ghosts in the deserts of Itabira
breeding shadows of the long-gone dead,
if my grandmother's hand
felt anything like this.

Clear Windows

What can be seen through windows in airports
without square frames, without names?
I watch the planes empty, not knowing how many hands

have touched this spot right here on the escalator
ascending toward the bare-white plastic ceiling.
Sometimes I think airports are like cathedrals

without the walls of red glass, cracked mass tabernacles.
In Florence, I saw thin, dancing skeletons painted on the dome,
and the windows had names because they were faces too,

and bodies, God dipped in the river,
Mary's tears in the Italian afternoon
like little bright jewels. In Florence,

there was no salt in the bread, so I spat
it out and waited and noted *never
come back again*. I'm finding it hard to believe

in what I haven't lived through.
I can't say what I felt when I learned
that most modern Japanese cities are made of stone

and steel because nothing wooden survived
the war. I know nothing is all surface
or substance but something in-between.

I'm trying to live through the things I believe.
That there's a difference between real and imagined
reasons for leaving something behind.

I grew up half-blind in a wooden house, not far
from the airport, planes passing overhead but never
close like this, the white cabins tucking themselves

away behind the glass, so far away they must be flying,
so still like an uncracked lake, I must be at the bottom.

Lost and Found

Leaving Philadelphia

I forget who told me to make the best of empty space.
It will only get emptier.
The way a mouth deprived, dried-out
in thirst, feels ten-times its size.
The blank walls of 320 felt like this some days:
unvarnished inkblot weighing down
the wood grain wallpaper.
Empty rooms where I learned
that brain bliss is all *unraveling*.
Word from root, tooth from toothache.
The first was "originate," my scabbed hands tracing the names
I'd carved into the hardwood dining table at seventeen—
ten years felt all at once.
I felt the dry rivers wondering why
they hadn't healed over after all this time.
No glossy amber pearls to poke open,
dig into tree-sap scabs, so long ago,
letters don't even come out of us
the same way anymore.
First lesson in forgetting: how even our resin rests unchallenged
like a blotter marking collapse of cause into event.
I forget who told me what it meant
to delight on rainy days:
If you can do it then, you can do it anytime.
Of course they meant *endure*
even when shit's rough cause some moments entrap

like flashfloods right before they buckle at their edges,
the way parkway peaks seem
to lead directly into vast gulfs of gray cloud
before the last rays of sun poke back
from near-distant New York glass.
It's not so sad
to drop "avuncular"
after Mom's voice falls away over the TV.
Not so hard to not pry
about the near-paradox of orphaned parents.
Some silences spill open
into erasure
once they're cracked.
When I was ten, we would spot rainbow trout
in the stream-thin tributary of Passaic
behind Aunt Lidia's weedy yard.
Even when her kids changed the locks of her little house,
heavy with the weight of antique stone heads,
we scaled slate steps to get there.
I forgot the word "pharyngeal" as soon as I learned
it was the size of a marble in the back of her throat.
The word dropped from my tongue,
became itself by melting away into larger leavings.
Mass atrophy of meaning until the mind was thin
enough to bear its own weight.
I forget why we kept going back to that river once she died,
once we knew not a single rainbow trout ever swam there,
that it was all mud-sucking carp
coughing up factory runoff.
Or I refused to believe hurt could only burn

into blue or bloom
into wound.
The way empty space empties,
a stone wants to be a stone.
Every wound wants to bloom
into its opposite,
roll back its birth,
lose itself so wholly
it can never be found.

A Good Thing

Evan, someone is knocking down the shallow
shelter of aspen woods by Washington School,
limb by limp limb.

And its rows of white
bannisters, pitched with dark
like a wilderness of hollow ribs,

can't remember the way you lay
in their curve, gulped boiling black
air, kicked chain-link and linty gin shooters

into shards of starry glass.
Every cell that swelled here, your breath heaving
in retreat, every auburn crest of a new bruise,
every ache as ache broke into ache, is gone.

Evan, there is no reason return arrives
with its crooked circles and decked ochre
like a cluster of gnat static in your ear.

Anatomies of Disappearance

There is no reason to avoid the smooth rain
of your old voice, no reason to care if it dissolves

into decay, a thin piece of tissue paper
melting on a tongue. He can say your name
all he wants. This is not a distance he can cross.

The next time I see you

we're gonna go to that bodega
where you buy Ferrero Rochers
for your mom. The same one where
that homeless lady called your hair
beautiful and blessed you
with a thousand angels
then proceeded to name them all aloud.
By the thirteenth, we just let her
do her thing. Clutching each other,
we quietly left, took a hard turn against
the brute wind on Concourse,
the sidewalk so blasted by sunglare
we almost gave up on dinner
and turned back toward home.
This time, we'll skip Joyce Kilmer's
crowned buds, let the nightlight moon's
neon blue lead the way back
to the woman, her gray tattered
jacket regal beside the brown
of the counter. I hope she's still
there, still chanting, and that she
hasn't run out of angels.

Franz Seigel Salsa

The workers are on strike somewhere,
but the dancers go on anyway,
despite the overgrown grass.
For a second, we pause, at first
to look through the fruit stand,
always in search of the perfect
rosebud-plump peach
when the sound hits us.
There they are—legs and leathern
brows beating back the heat
as if the street around
were raising them above
the world where we stand
planted. It's automatic, the way
you move in an arc toward me,
softly lilting like southern air.
For a split second, we're alone
half-naked in the low light
of your room but raised too
with the other dancers.
My hands find your turning sides,
knees bent in repose, twisting
with my hips before
the red light lifts
your hand to mine.

Like Sun Through a Bent Sky

The change began with thousands of heads
askew, moving in and out of the sun,
floating above the sidewalks and crossways—
not floating exactly but caught
in a drift that bent things away
from each other.

Let me explain: I was in midtown, fleeing
3 o'clock on the wrong line,
emerging with only the wish for empty
land or an empty mind,
finding instead the Bank of America
tower and gyro plumes, sunglasses, bloody little pins,
and curling smoke, insidious like the begged air
that broke this year
into smaller and smaller pieces
of sad and incontrovertible truths.

My body has been in 20 states this year,
bent on its reader's hook.
Has cried maybe 40 times,
grown tombstones
like barnacles, swallowed words whole
to keep peace.

So, what reversed exactly
away from that metal thumb, walking back
toward Harlem, along Malcolm X boulevard,
was of no consequence inasmuch
as a blossom is a consequence of season
emerging so softly in its endless
repetition, maybe what changed was in me
this little engine among engines
knowing or not knowing
how one could be delivered
from another.

How one could walk from midtown to Harlem
along Malcolm X boulevard, how one could walk
does walk, walks every day or doesn't walk, never walks,
will never walk from the site of one life and another
so culled and questioned, space bent along imaginary lines
into harsher and harsher shapes. Not knowing how these heads
surrender each day the only way
they can. Not in prayer but continuing
to bend toward convergence—

I am trying to say I am trying
to love as many people as I can
the only way I know how,
the hardest way.
That in trying I found only this feeling
so large and absent
and vital, like the city itself were built
on a dried-out riverbed, bound forever
by an absence.

An Example of Universal Language

Take the barkless branch ripped from its own skin.
Its scarry rivers and capillary paths where ants carve
their own dead language into the dead wood.
Yesterday is a soup of these dead languages. This wrinkle
cresting over your eye, these formless letters, could
be fault lines. One meaning couched in another.
Like this Hungarian lard, this sugar lump, this apology
for others who cannot. Maybe I'll never trace Concourse Ivy
again. It's dominoes, it's conciliatory delights. Remember
that shadow in the shape of a balloon cast on the courthouse
wall? It was July; it was a soup of languages that managed
to survive. All around us the sound of phones erasing time
like little bleak lighters. And we could never make out
the origin of that shape. Like a ghost or a stain. Or a belief.

Warsaw, NC

We come across an orphaned church
shipwrecked on a patch of swamp.
Black hunting nests necking the flooded timber.

The trees wane into white shadow.
Mauve sheet of sky hums from its overhead throat.
The flowers float lower, white eyes in the water.

Loblolly poplar and sweetgum spread
in daisy dust pockets along the flat end.
A bumperless car is slumped over its spilt teeth.

A body's head rippling in the windshield
pulls an anxious silk thread
from my toe, drags it along

until something unravels, curls,
glows like a tail in the damp sky.

The Willows

Something Happened in Cape Fear

They lined the highway that crossed from Virginia into Carolina,
arching up from the blue-black fray of open land
like old, massive skeletons.

Only time I'd pictured a willow was heartsick, listening to Patsy Cline,
and I don't think they looked quite like the real thing.
Black mangled arms giving in alms threads of gold light,
ghost-gray hair hanging in wavy spindles like falling smoke.

I woke as we soared through steel-towns
with rusted-shut porno theaters,
old barns bulging with black oak.
Past Roanoke-Rapids and the motel I'd booked
then cancelled two years before when I loved someone
whom I no longer love,
planning a route to Colombia.

I was with my father; we were talking about marriage.
He asked if I planned on marrying multiple people
because I'd said *whomever they might be.*

Evan Dekens

The subject changed; we played Styx on the radio.
I was grateful for the kitsch synth as I split,
as in willingly displaced,
simultaneously beside him and somewhere else,
somewhere between the big alien trees
passing on either side and the broad sunny beams of light
they'd carved onto the road.

I saw how each arm bent wildly up and away
from origin on its own crooked path like a family.

How wayward was my own that first night? The group of us a crush
crammed on the sidewalk, half-drunk listening to K— drone
on about the ghosts he saw sometimes dancing stiff with the breeze.

I turned away and imagined the bodies hanging before the high windows
winking Christmas lights that shone in every one of those restored homes
and how little is known of the felt reality before
only old, leftover fragments woven into record and recompense.

A certain mythmaking is involved in starting over.
Take the Gullah, who in forced homelessness,
made home out of baskets woven by hand
and sold in huts whose old remains I saw

on the long highway drive to Charleston,
passing on either side with shocking regularity.

Cropped up next door were luxury rental villages,
each with a name like *colonial plantation* or *plantation village*
with khaki and hack molding mounted beneath the sign.

About leaving: you look at skies differently.
Not as a sea of old light but a ribbon of space,

a river of time connecting two distant points,
a reminder of distance's influence, how it warps,

wavers in delay behind the skyline's gothic churches
and cherub marsh. Above metric tons of swamp

mush melting beyond the last lonely, flooded pines of town—
constellations brighter than I'd ever known.
Never saw country as open to abandon as this.

Born so tightly packed, stars barely bled
through the sky blighted with New York light.

In Carolina, I learned there is no edge
of time marking when one year or minute

or moment ceases to seem real, stacked in continuum against relentless
river winds. I know and I don't know what happened in Cape Fear.

Two rememberings ripping each other along seams stitched with silences.
I know somewhere in the suburbs there were sad eyes watching Castle street

lined on each side with pastel and the smell of coffee
run by transplant white kids from the college,
rent climbing like a dragnet across each new hipster storefront—
all erasing with lent, the gentrified scent of a blooming that always buries.

Driving down Fullerton, I read the message: *something happened*
scrawled on the lamppost over and over and over until the words stuck.

What happened sixty feet away, two hundred years ago
was bullets and burnt hope, cracked eardrums
and scabbed, wooded beams where we, you, I, He, She

dove whole bright tracts of time into dead futures
scattered fractal families, chewed homes with fire and smoke that rose
and still rises and still rests in the Cape Fear River,

its coasts slowly being eaten by the current,
the city washing away its own name to escape.

I once thought places existed in varying degrees
of realness, that one really could couch

collectives of time bleeding differently into history
than others, that richer sunshine or pitch sky scattered
with sapphire was somehow heavier than what I had.

That this city rests on a river run to sea,
a constant witness to retreat must explain

the way these trees have grown at angles
with the wind. Wicked, salt-bleached

by echo, Fort Fisher—calmer than the miniature
diorama, calm voice explaining how

the confederates couldn't hold out,
how the south fell a few weeks after,

that each square foot of beach is bled deep
with open mouths and old rain and thank God
they can't eat or speak anymore.

Psalm for the Unuttered

Why do we write our lives
as if they are not white?
A story told of families,
fights, faces—the unuttered,
not containing enough space
for each forgotten name.
When I was young,
I told this story to myself, about myself,
all around like still, falling fog:
you are the story that is being told
you are the story that is being told
you are the story that is being told

Against Confession

Here is the poem I'm not old enough to write
where I've watched decades pass and people
change—where I remember laughing under scattered
string-lit bars with scores of friends who've since died
or moved. Where I recall packing up my life several times
and heading West into California's wildfire riffraff, staggering
my way along confused backstreets until I found home
or a metaphor for home
in some drink
halfway
to death
you
expect to find the mythic South here with its back-porches
and ghosts like the sounds of vanished gun barrels gone cold
in the clay earth. Where there was a girl—and yes, I do mean a girl,
a white girl, but I won't say she's white, you'll assume, and she will
do tragic things to my heart. Or so I will write—of ghastly, gnashing
insanity of loneliness beyond lone flooded pines, caught in pitch
with choruses of toads and owls and drunk drivers running the road.
And I will be old and sad that the world where I learned to love
by never getting any
has vanished.
But I am 22
or 24—the years stop feeling like years after 20.
I've traveled a bit, never as far as Ho Chi Minh or Bogota,
never seen the sun on Angolan sand or tasted Italian

soil. This is the real poem—the one where I'm reaching
with both hands and scraping dangerously at the skin above my skin
where I've written all my other works. And I spend the weekends with
a woman I love, who loves me, and there's no tragedy in either of us
save for our own private pasts—only hard because we're human,
and human work is unending, impossible, but fuels weekends full
of warm curling-up between plush quilts. And endless trips to Shop-Rite
to buy salmon, spinach, marzipan, fiber soda, plantains, cheese, baguettes
shipped in from Brooklyn, mushrooms—bought and paid by jobs that pay
too little, afforded by lives shaped by parents with money. This is the poem
where I grew up hating the rich, afraid of the poor, wrathful of the dumb,
numb to beauty or tears—the one where I learn the hard way what
money wrought in the North Jersey towns where my brothers
and I lived and lied to each other about where we went
when we left the house. Where I, hunched and thin, read nearly
every word I've ever read and roasted chickens with potatoes and carrots
where the world was one big white poem. It's the kind of poem you write
accidentally, unwillingly, sewn into every story you try to tell—the one where
you've lost loved ones
willingly, abandoned friends,
been haunted by them
along with lovers and pasts
where your mind
was younger, leaner
bred with balance and strange ambition
and maybe fed by loneliness, and maybe stoned with self-apathy. It's the poem
that forgives nothing, leaves nothing, must be covered up as best as one can
like a wound blown wide open to wind and rain, like the body you kept awake
with Hank Williams earworms, laying on the lowest hollow of a mountaintop
swaddled by rivulets of condensation, so thirsty you sucked the damp from

woodchips strewn on the ground. Where you still remember
days in the past where your teeth chattered with anxiety for hours
or when your legs were too heavy to lift, and now you swallow two miracles,
two pills each morning and feel calm nearly always.
The one where you learn to thrash your thoughts into submission with still
and forgiving—where you forgive yourself for everything. Where you invite frien
to your family's house and cook them curry labored over for hours,
    where some brilliant
days end with you and the woman you love curled up in a down-comforter,
and you both smell like cardamom, cinnamon, and dry smoke,
the smell of splitting wood with her by your side,
and no-one has died or drank themselves into liver failure.
You're all in the relative safety of the yard your father
still mows excitedly each weekend, and no-one is lost
far away or swallowed by the black bile of time,
the poem where you can gather everyone you love by a fire you've
made splitting logs to tinder and breathing it into life
against the night's crickets and owls and thick dark
you and the people you love
warm and safe by the light you've made
flickering, alive, from almost nothing.

Charleston Smooth

As we turn the corner, a man calls after us
asking if we're engaged. Save for a few
falling petals, everything conspires to form

the scene. A wedding ceremony opens
into the street. White coverlets and stiff
coattails muffle the murmur of waiters

wandering through the venue patio
and into the street. The trees wiry with invisible
weight weaving their ancient limbs

through the teeth of gravestones like looms.
You and I, elbows clamped tight,
shake our heads *No. Not engaged.*

The man presses to ask
if we're on our honeymoon.
We laugh

but don't speak,
allowing the walk away
under the canopies

of mouth-shaped leaves
grating the sunset into coins
of mauve light,

the soft tap of our feet
fading into waves
of sound,

our soft steps,
our light laughter,
our answer.

Acknowledgments

I'd like to thank first and foremost all of the teachers, professors, and guides I've had throughout my life, most notably Melissa Crowe and Patricia Matthew for encouraging and guiding me to become the writer and thinker I am today. And to my students, whether in Newark or Wilmington, guiding you as writers has never ceased to remind me of why I started in the first place.

I'd like to thank my family, and my parents. So much of this collection (not to mention *my whole life*) would not have been possible without the life you've provided for me. I will always be thankful for that.

Thank you to all the folks in Wilmington, both professors and peers, who were among the first readers of *Anatomies of Disappearance*'s earliest poems. And to my friends who have always supported me in writing, and in life–Sarah, Luke (everyone on the poetry ws chain), Liam, the other Liam, Chris, Tim, Lee (everyone in Sunday Dinner), and Steve. Thank you to my brothers Nick and Michael.

I want to thank Crystal, who inspired many of these poems and gave me the confidence to write them. She is always the first reader, and the first fan of my writing, as I am of hers.

This collection came together during a period of time when I was working in the Ironbound section of Newark, commuting along the passaic river each morning, feeling defeated by my year-long stint in the south and at a loss for which path to take forward. When I found that path in the

43

very place I had so enthusiastically fled, it rooted me deeply in a sense of community, duty, humility, and belonging. I have to thank this place, New Jersey, from the bubble of affluence where I was born, to the cafes and bookstores of Montclair where I live, to the dusty streets of Newark where I found my purpose, my community. All of these places live in me, my home, now and forever.

About the Author

Evan Dekens was born and raised in New Jersey. He received degrees in English and Transformative Urban Education from Montclair State University and briefly studied fiction writing in the University of North Carolina Wilmington's MFA program. After leaving the program, he dedicated his work primarily to education and poetry. His criticism, reviews, and poetry appear or are forthcoming in *The Humanities Review*, *FilmMatters*, and *Public Books*. He lives in Montclair NJ with his partner, and is proud to work in Newark where he teaches English and Creative Writing at Arts High School.

Comparable April Gloaming Titles

the anonym gospels by Em J Parsley

Birds of Sympathy: Correspondences by Douglas Smith & George Looney

The Mustard Seed by Sugar la Fae

All Things Holy and Heathen by Chelsea Jackson

Rituals by Lorcan Black